NEBRASKA CORNHUSKERS

BY
MARGARET WEBER

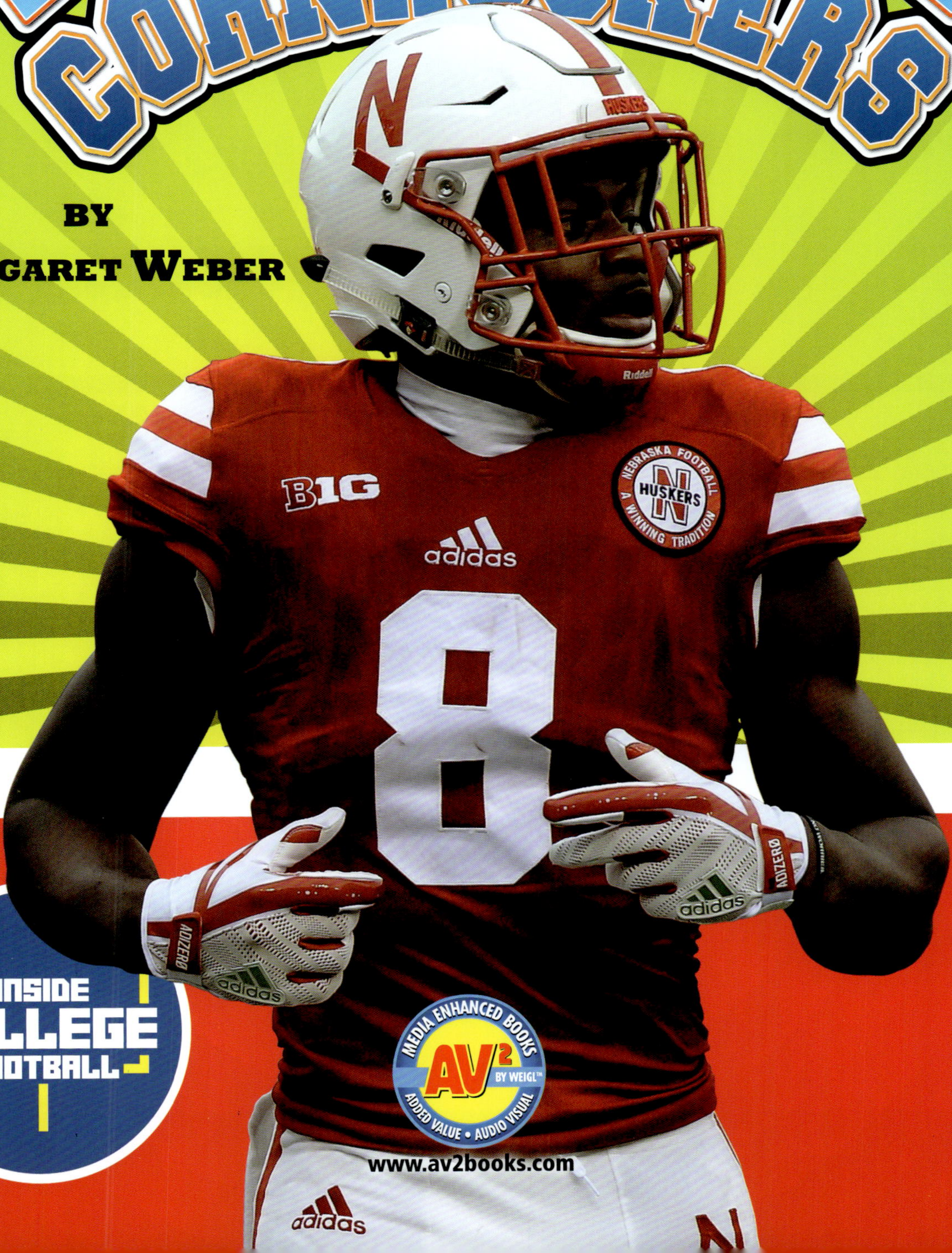

INSIDE COLLEGE FOOTBALL

MEDIA ENHANCED BOOKS
AV² BY WEIGL™
ADDED VALUE • AUDIO VISUAL

www.av2books.com

Published by AV² by Weigl
350 5th Avenue, 59th Floor
New York, NY 10118
Website: www.av2books.com

Library of Congress Control Number: 2018968214

ISBN 978-1-7911-0114-5 (hardcover)
ISBN 978-1-7911-0115-2 (multi-user eBook)
ISBN 978-1-7911-0116-9 (single-user eBook)

Printed in Guangzhou, China
1 2 3 4 5 6 7 8 9 0 23 22 21 20 19

042019
102318

Project Coordinator: Jared Siemens Designer: Terry Paulhus

Every reasonable effort has been made to trace ownership and to obtain permission to reprint copyright material. The publishers would be pleased to have any errors or omissions brought to their attention so that they may be corrected in subsequent printings.

The publisher acknowledges Alamy, Getty Images, and Wikimedia Commons as its primary image suppliers for this title.

Nebraska Cornhuskers

CONTENTS

Introduction

The University of Nebraska–Lincoln is home to the Cornhuskers. The football team first played in 1890. Since then, the Cornhuskers have become one of the greatest teams in college football. They hold five national titles. The Cornhuskers are ranked fourth for most wins of all time in college football. After the 2017 season, Nebraska had a total of 893 wins. This is a legacy the Cornhuskers strive to continue.

The Cornhuskers are also known for their **rivalries** against fellow Midwestern states, such as Iowa and Minnesota. All three teams are part of the Big Ten Conference. The University of Nebraska–Lincoln joined the conference in the 2011 season. Whenever the Cornhuskers play against Iowa or Minnesota, they compete for trophies. These trophies are held by the winning team until they meet again. The Cornhuskers remain competitive as they look for a championship finish in the Big Ten and a spot in the nation's top 25.

When Brenden Jaimes started in Nebraska's 2017 game against the Rutgers University Scarlet Knights, he was only the fifth true-freshman offensive linemen in history to start for the Cornhuskers.

Running back Maurice Washington finished the 2018 season with 676 total yards and four touchdowns. Washington earned the second-highest total receptions of any true freshman in Nebraska history, with 24 total receptions in 11 games.

NEBRASKA

Stadium Memorial Stadium

Division Big Ten West

Head Coach Scott Frost

Location Lincoln, Nebraska

National Championships 5

Nicknames Cornhuskers, 'Huskers

5
Official Fight Songs

25
Retired Jerseys

359
NFL Draft Picks

3
Heisman Memorial Trophy Winners

History

In 1892, George Flippin became the **first African American** to play for the Cornhuskers.

Although he stepped down as head coach of the Cornhuskers in 1972, Bob Devaney continued to serve as Nebraska's athletic director until 1993.

On November 27, 1890, the University of Nebraska–Lincoln fielded its first football team. Although the game was shorter in length and the rules varied from today's game, this was the true beginning of Cornhuskers football. After playing for three years, the team became more organized. Frank Crawford was hired as the very first coach in 1893. The team had many early successes. These included a 24-game winning streak between 1902 and 1905.

The years after World War I (1914–1918) marked a new era of football for the Cornhuskers. After the war, the team brought new excitement to Nebraska. In 1921, the Cornhuskers won every game except for one loss against the University of Notre Dame Fighting Irish. However, from the 1940s to the 1960s, the Cornhuskers struggled to complete winning seasons.

When Bob Devaney came to Nebraska in 1962, the Cornhuskers returned to the successful team fans knew and loved. The Cornhuskers won nine games and only lost two during the 1962 season. This marked the beginning of 40 **consecutive** seasons during which the team ended with more wins than losses. In recent years, the Cornhuskers have had both winning and losing seasons. Between 2008 and 2014, the team ended each season with 9 or 10 wins. Today, Nebraska looks to recapture another decades-long winning streak.

Before they were known as the Cornhuskers, Nebraska football players were called the "Old Gold Knights" and the "Bugeaters."

The Stadium

Only two cities in the state of Nebraska, Lincoln and Omaha, have a larger population than a sold-out Memorial Stadium.

The Nebraska Cornhuskers play at Memorial Stadium in Lincoln, Nebraska. The stadium is known as one of the "Cathedrals of College Football" by *Sporting News*. It is widely considered to be one of the most intimidating stadiums in all of college football. Fans know it by the nickname the "Boneyard." On game days, the stadium is awash in red as fans gather to cheer on the Cornhuskers.

Memorial Stadium was built in 1923. The stadium has undergone many changes as the popularity of football and the Cornhuskers continues to grow. The official capacity of the stadium is 85,458. However, crowds regularly exceed 90,000 for home games. Nebraska holds the National Collegiate Athletic Association (NCAA) record for sold-out crowds. Since 1962, there have been 368 consecutive sold-out home games at the stadium.

There have been many improvements to the stadium through construction and additions. In the 1960s and 1970s, there were multiple expansions to secure additional permanent seating. In 1999, **luxury** boxes were added. Before the 2006 season, the Tom and Nancy Osborne Athletic Complex was constructed. Each improvement has made Memorial Stadium a more exciting place to watch Cornhuskers football.

Regardless of the game's outcome, Nebraska fans stand and applaud the visiting team as they leave the field after every game in Memorial Stadium.

Where They Play

Welcome to Memorial Stadium. Die-hard fans turn out rain or shine to cheer on their team. For almost a century, crowds of 90,000 or more have filled the stadium for home football games. A winning team, a top marching band, and many fan traditions make Memorial Stadium one of college football's best.

BIG TEN WEST

1 **Northwestern University**
Evanston, Illinois

2 **Purdue University**
West Lafayette, Indiana

3 **University of Illinois**
Urbana-Champaign, Illinois

4 **University of Iowa**
Iowa City, Iowa

5 **University of Minnesota**
Minneapolis, Minnesota

★6 **University of Nebraska**
Lincoln, Nebraska

7 **University of Wisconsin**
Madison, Wisconsin

Arena
Memorial Stadium

Location
Lincoln, Nebraska

Broke Ground
April 26, 1923

Completed
October 20, 1923

Surface
Artificial Turf

Features
- Two 17-foot (5-meter) tall replay boards
- Statue of Coach Bob Devaney is located outside the stadium
- Four verses of prose written for the team mark each corner of the stadium

BIG TEN EAST

1 **Indiana University**
Bloomington, Indiana

2 **Michigan State University**
East Lansing, Michigan

3 **Ohio State University**
Columbus, Ohio

4 **Pennsylvania State University**
State College, Pennsylvania

5 **Rutgers University–New Brunswick**
New Brunswick–Piscataway, New Jersey

6 **University of Maryland**
College Park, Maryland

7 **University of Michigan**
Ann Arbor, Michigan

NORTH DAKOTA
MINNESOTA
SOUTH DAKOTA
WISCONSIN
MICHIGAN
NEW YORK
RHODE ISLAND
CONNECTICUT
PENNSYLVANIA
NEW JERSEY
IOWA
NEBRASKA
ILLINOIS
INDIANA
OHIO
DELAWARE
MARYLAND
WASHINGTON, D.C.
WEST VIRGINIA
VIRGINIA
KANSAS
MISSOURI
KENTUCKY
NORTH CAROLINA
TENNESSEE
SOUTH CAROLINA
OKLAHOMA
ARKANSAS
MISSISSIPPI
ALABAMA
GEORGIA
Atlantic Ocean
TEXAS
LOUISIANA
FLORIDA
Gulf of Mexico
SCALE
0 miles
500 miles
0 kilometers
500 km
LEGEND
Home Stadium
Big Ten West
Big Ten East
United States
Other Countries
Water

The Uniforms

In 2018, the Cornhuskers wore helmets that were designed to look like the original leather helmets worn after **World War I.**

The University of Nebraska collaborated with Adidas to create a throwback uniform that honored many Cornhuskers traditions. The numbers and fonts on the players' jerseys were inspired by the original clock that hung in Memorial Stadium in 1923.

The Nebraska Cornhuskers wear scarlet and cream. Scarlet is a specific shade of red. Cream is a specific shade of white. Both the home and away helmets are cream with a scarlet "N" on the side. The two standard uniforms are opposite versions of each other. The scarlet home jerseys have cream lettering and are paired with cream pants. Previous versions included a scarlet stripe. The stripes were removed in 2018 for a cleaner look. The cream away jersey has scarlet lettering that is paired with scarlet pants.

HOME

AWAY

The Cornhuskers wear alternate uniforms for special occasions. In 2018, the Cornhuskers celebrated the anniversary of their first season at Memorial Stadium. In honor of the 1923 season, the team wore jerseys that resembled those worn when the stadium was built. The jerseys had lettering and patterns reminiscent of the era. Alternate jerseys remind the team and fans of their history.

In 2018, Coach Scott Frost added each player's home area code to the front of his helmet to remind them that they represent their hometowns as well as the University of Nebraska when they take the field.

Student Athletes

The Cornhuskers have one of the **highest graduation rates** for football players in the Big Ten Conference, second only to Northwestern University.

Adrian Martinez became the first true freshman quarterback to start a season opener for the Cornhuskers in 2018. Martinez was named a Freshman All-American and was listed on Nebraska's Scholar-Athlete Honor Roll.

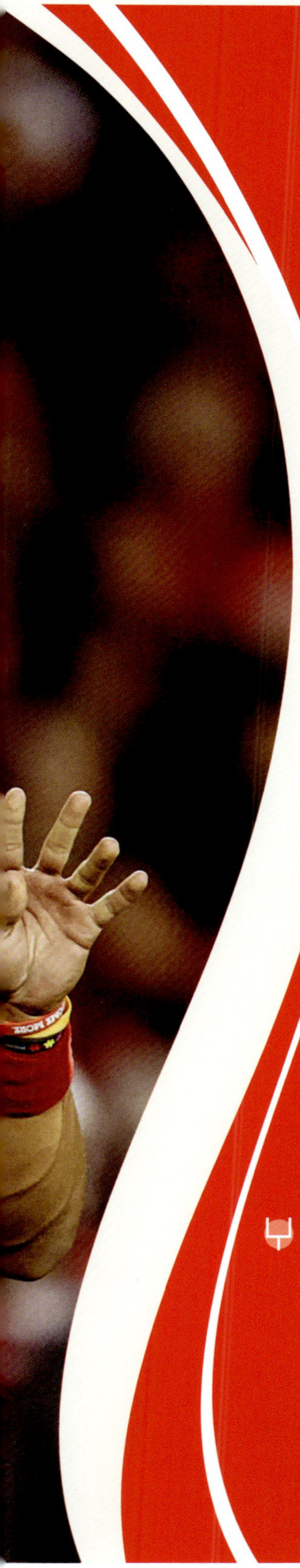

Being a college student athlete is hard work. Student athletes have to perform well on the football field and in the classroom. Nebraska student athletes are required to meet a minimum grade point average and attend all of their classes. They must also have 12 academic credits per term.

Many student athletes are given athletic scholarships. A scholarship is a financial aid agreement between the athlete and the university. Athletes who do not receive an athletic scholarship can be "walk-on" members of the team. This means they are on the team, but without athletic financial aid. The University of Nebraska typically awards the maximum number of football scholarships allowed, which is 85.

The University of Nebraska also has a program for all student athletes called Post-Eligibility Opportunities (PEO). This program helps student athletes find internships, study abroad, or continue on to graduate school. The PEO program is designed to help student athletes take the skills they learn as both students and athletes into their futures.

Wide receiver JD Spielman holds multiple Nebraska records, and his on-field performance includes a 21-game reception streak. Off the field, Spielman has been on the Nebraska Scholar-Athlete Honor Roll.

Bowl Games

From 1969 to 2003, Nebraska appeared in **35 consecutive bowl games,** setting an NCAA record.

The Cornhuskers defeated the University of California, Los Angeles Bruins 37–29 in the 2015 Foster Farms Bowl. Played in Santa Clara, California, just south of San Francisco, the bowl's trophy features San Francisco's famous Golden Gate Bridge.

Bowl Games are a unique sports tradition in college football. In the beginning of college football, there was no true **postseason**. Today, a variety of postseason bowl games are played. Bowl games give teams the opportunity to continue striving for recognition and victory after the end of regular play. There are currently 40 bowl games played in various combinations each year. These games are chosen with input from teams, sponsors, and the College Football Playoff Selection Committee. The game **matchups** are announced in December.

Fans of the Cornhuskers have enjoyed many postseason games with their team. The Cornhuskers have the fifth-most appearances in bowl games of any team in college football. Their first bowl game was the Rose Bowl, when they played Stanford University. The Cornhuskers have played in a total of 53 bowl games.

The 2016 Music City Bowl was the third meeting between the Cornhuskers and the University of Tennessee Volunteers. Although Nebraska was victorious in the previous games, the 1998 Orange Bowl and the 2000 Fiesta Bowl, Tennessee defeated the 'Huskers 38–24 at the Music City Bowl.

The Coaches

After his coaching career, **Tom Osborne** represented Nebraska's Third District in the U.S. House of Representatives between 2001 and 2007.

Scott Frost was the starting quarterback for Nebraska's 1997 National Championship team. Although his first season as Nebraska's head coach ended with a 4–8 record, Frost fostered a bond with his players throughout the season that laid the foundation for future winning seasons.

There have been 31 head coaches in Nebraska history. Some of these coaches only stayed for a season or two. This includes many of the team's early coaches. It wasn't until 1900 that a coach served for more than two years. Other coaches spent many years coaching Nebraska football. Each coach helped to shape the football team and the way the Cornhuskers play today.

BOB DEVANEY When Bob Devaney came to Nebraska in 1962, the team was ready for a new coach after seven consecutive losing seasons. Right away, Devaney made a difference. Nebraska began to win consistently again. In 1970, 1971, and 1972, Devaney led the Cornhuskers to three-straight Orange Bowl victories. He retired in 1972 with a 136–30–7 overall record.

TOM OSBORNE Tom Osborne was the **offensive coordinator** for the Cornhuskers under Devaney and became head coach after Devaney retired. Osborne proved himself a consistent and dedicated coach. Under his leadership, the Cornhuskers won nine or more games every season. He brought National Championships and conference championships home to Lincoln. Osborne coached at Nebraska from 1973 to 1997, and was **inducted** into the College Football **Hall of Fame** in 1999.

SCOTT FROST Scott Frost was already a familiar face to Nebraska fans when he became head coach in 2017. Frost played for the Cornhuskers under Tom Osborne. He is known for throwing a famous pass that turned into a touchdown and win for the Cornhuskers. That game sealed the team's number-one ranking in 1997. Frost also brings National Football League (NFL) playing and coaching experience to Nebraska.

The Mascot

Since 2003, Herbie Husker usually wears a red collared shirt, but sometimes trades it for a Cornhuskers jersey when he poses with fans at football games.

The University of Nebraska–Lincoln did not settle on the Cornhuskers name until the year 1900. Originally known as the Bugeaters, the team was first called the Cornhuskers by sportswriter Cy Sherman. Unlike other teams, there is no official symbol to represent a Cornhusker. It refers to someone who removes the husk from corn. Corn has always been an important crop grown in the state of Nebraska.

Herbie Husker was the first mascot to represent the team. He was created in 1974. Herbie Husker represents the typical Nebraskan. He wears work jeans, a red shirt, and a cowboy hat with the "N" **logo**. Herbie has an oversized, cartoonish human head. A second mascot, Lil' Red, joined the team in 1993. He is a young man dressed in red overalls and a red cap.

Lil' Red has the personality of a young child and is meant to appeal to younger Cornhuskers fans. His main job is to make people laugh.

Legends of the Past

For many players, their time with the Cornhuskers is the start of a promising football career. These are some of the best-known football players to play for the University of Nebraska–Lincoln.

Sam Koch

Sam Koch was a walk-on player for the Nebraska Cornhuskers in 2002. That year, he was the backup punter. He received a scholarship and became the team's primary punter in 2004. In 2005, his punting average was 46.5 yards. This was a single-season record for the team. During Koch's senior year, he was nominated for the Ray Guy Award. He also had eight punts with an average of 51.5 yards during the Alamo Bowl against the University of Michigan. He caught the attention of the Baltimore Ravens and was **drafted** into the NFL in 2006, where he still plays today.

Position: Punter
Seasons: 2002–2005 (Nebraska Cornhuskers), 2006–Present (Baltimore Ravens)
Born: August 13, 1982, York, Nebraska

Prince Amukamara

Prince Amukamara arrived at the University of Nebraska in 2007. As a freshman, Amukamara played in eight games. As a sophomore, he became a valuable player for the team and played in all 13 regular-season games. During a game against the Western Michigan University Broncos, Amukamara made eight tackles, his high point of the 2008 season. While playing for the Cornhuskers, he was recognized as a finalist for the Jim Thorpe Award. He joined the NFL in 2011 and currently plays for the Chicago Bears.

Position: Cornerback
Seasons: 2007–2010 (Nebraska Cornhuskers), 2011–2015 (New York Giants), 2016 (Jacksonville Jaguars), 2017–Present (Chicago Bears)
Born: June 6, 1989, Leominster, Massachusetts

Lavonte David

Lavonte David did not start his college career in Nebraska. Before transferring to join the Cornhuskers, David attended Fort Scott Community College, where he also played football. During his first year as a Cornhusker, he made 152 total tackles. This was a record for Nebraska. David started in all 27 games he played during the two years he was on the team. He also holds the Cornhuskers record for most tackles made by a two-year player. Today, he plays for the Tampa Bay Buccaneers after being drafted into the NFL in 2012.

Position: Outside Linebacker
Seasons: 2010–2011 (Nebraska Cornhuskers), 2012–Present (Tampa Bay Buccaneers)
Born: January 23, 1990, Miami, Florida

Nathan Gerry

Fans of the Nebraska Cornhuskers watched Nathan Gerry on the field for four seasons after he joined the team in 2013. As a linebacker, he had 32 tackles in his freshman year. This was a promising start that Gerry made into a successful college career. Gerry started every game in 2015. He was also named to both the second and third All-Big Ten teams. In 2017, he was drafted by the Philadelphia Eagles. He played with the Eagles when they won **Super Bowl** LII in 2018.

Position: Linebacker
Seasons: 2013–2016 (Nebraska Cornhuskers), 2017–Present (Philadelphia Eagles)
Born: February 23, 1995, Sioux Falls, South Dakota

All-Time Records

12

Single-Season Receiving Touchdowns

Quincy Enunwa holds the record for most receiving touchdowns as a Cornhusker, with 12 in the 2013 season.

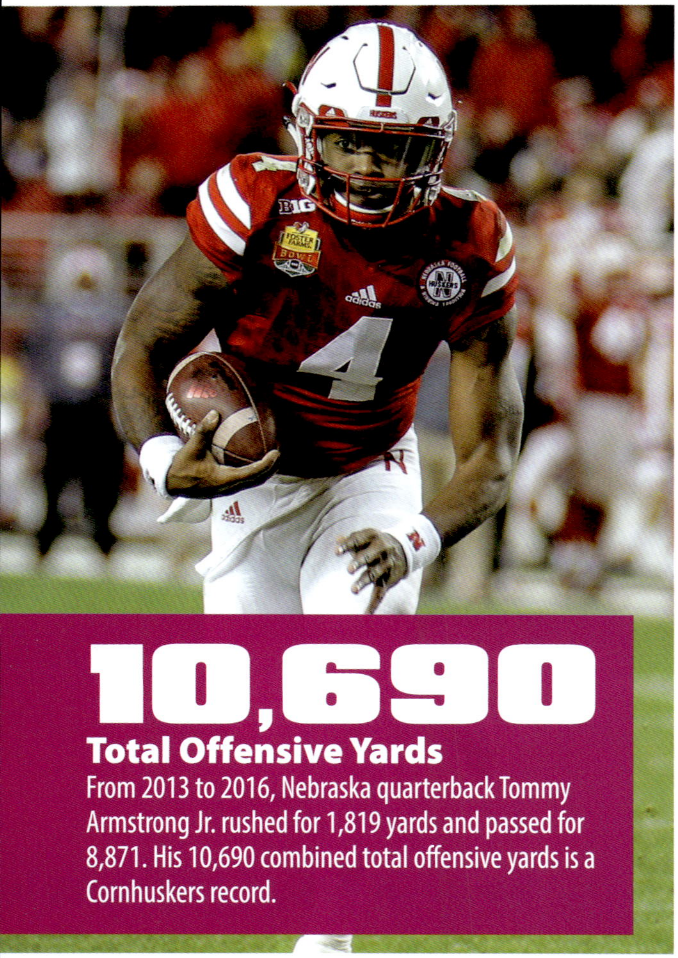

10,690

Total Offensive Yards

From 2013 to 2016, Nebraska quarterback Tommy Armstrong Jr. rushed for 1,819 yards and passed for 8,871. His 10,690 combined total offensive yards is a Cornhuskers record.

91,585

Single-Game Attendance

'Huskers fans set the record for attendance at Memorial Stadium in 2014, when 91,585 people cheered Nebraska to a 41–31 win over the University of Miami Hurricanes.

95

Longest Rushing Touchdown

In September 2001, Eric Crouch set the all-time record for the longest rushing touchdown against the University of Missouri Tigers, at 95 yards.

63

Most Points in a Half

The Cornhuskers set a record for most points scored in a half in September 1995, with 63 in a game against the Arizona State University Sun Devils.

Timeline

Throughout the team's history, the Nebraska Cornhuskers have had many memorable events that have become defining moments for the team and its fans.

In 1901, the Cornhuskers begin what will become a 24-straight game-winning streak.

1890
Nebraska takes the field for the first time against a team representing a YMCA from Omaha.

1929–1936
Dana X. Bible coaches the Cornhuskers, during which time Nebraska claims six conference titles.

1900 | 1920 | 1940 | 1960

1962
Bob Devaney joins Nebraska as head coach, ushering in an exciting era of Cornhuskers football.

1971
"The Game of the Century" is played on November 25. The Cornhuskers beat the Oklahoma Sooners 35–31.

The Future

With a new coach leading the way, the Cornhuskers are poised to battle to the top of the Big Ten Conference. As a player under one of the team's greatest coaches, Frost knows what it means to carry on the traditions of the Nebraska Cornhuskers. With support from some of the most dedicated fans in college football, the future is bright in Lincoln.

1972

Bob Devaney steps down as head coach and hands the team over to one of his assistant coaches, Tom Osborne.

2017

Scott Frost returns to Nebraska, this time as a coach, to take on the top position for the Nebraska Cornhuskers.

1970 | 1980 | 2000 | 2020

1969–1972

The Cornhuskers win 32 games in a row.

In 1995, Nebraska wins back-to-back championships, making it the ninth team to do so in college football.

Write a Biography

Life Story

A person's life story can be the subject of a book. This kind of book is called a biography. Biographies often describe the lives of people who have achieved great success. These people may be alive today, or they may have lived many years ago. Reading a biography can help you learn more about a great person.

Get the Facts

Use this book, and research in the library and on the internet, to find out more about your favorite player. Learn as much about him as you can. What position does he play? What are his statistics in important categories? Has he set any records? Also, be sure to write down key events in the person's life. What was his childhood like? What has he accomplished off the field? Is there anything else that makes this person special or unusual?

Use the Concept Web

A concept web is a useful research tool. Read the questions in the concept web on the following page. Answer the questions in your notebook. Your answers will help you write a biography.

Concept Web

Write a Biography

Adulthood
- Where does this individual currently reside?
- Does he have a family?

Your Opinion
- What did you learn from the books you read in your research?
- Would you suggest these books to others?
- Was anything missing from these books?

Childhood
- Where and when was this person born?
- Describe his parents, siblings, and friends.
- Did he grow up in unusual circumstances?

Accomplishments off the Field
- What is this person's life's work?
- Has he received awards or recognition for accomplishments?
- How have this person's accomplishments served others?

Help and Obstacles
- Did this individual have a positive attitude?
- Did he receive help from others?
- Did this person have a mentor?
- Did this person face any hardships?
- If so, how were the hardships overcome?

Accomplishments on the Field
- What records does this person hold?
- What key games and plays have defined his career?
- What are his stats in categories important to his position?

Work and Preparation
- What was this person's education?
- What was his work experience?
- How does this person work?
- What is the process he uses?

Trivia Time

Take this quiz to test your knowledge of the Nebraska Cornhuskers. The answers are printed upside down under each question.

1 In what year did the Cornhuskers first play football?

A. 1890

2 When was Nebraska's first season in the Big Ten?

A. 2011

3 How many jerseys has the team retired?

A. 25

4 What was the Cornhuskers record in 1962?

A. 9–2

5 How many National Championships do the Cornhuskers hold?

A. Five

6 What is the nickname for Memorial Stadium?

A. The Boneyard

7 Who is the current coach of the Nebraska Cornhuskers?

A. Scott Frost

8 What colors represent the Cornhuskers?

A. Scarlet and cream

9 What are the names of the team's mascots?

A. Herbie Husker and Lil' Red

10 Which Cornhusker won the Super Bowl in 2018?

A. Nathan Gerry

Key Words

consecutive: following in an unbroken order

drafted: chosen to play professionally in the National Football League during an annual event

Hall of Fame: a group of persons judged to be outstanding in a particular sport

inducted: added as an official member of a group

logo: a symbol that stands for a team or organization

luxury: having great comfort and extravagance

matchups: contests between two athletes or sports teams

offensive coordinator: a coaching staff member of a gridiron football team who is in charge of the offense

postseason: a sporting event that takes place after the end of the regular season

rivalries: competitions between different groups or individuals toward the same objective or goal

Super Bowl: the NFL's annual championship game between the winning team from the National Football Conference and the winning team from the American Football Conference

Index

Log on to www.av2books.com

AV² by Weigl brings you media enhanced books that support active learning. Go to www.av2books.com, and enter the special code found on page 2 of this book. You will gain access to enriched and enhanced content that supplements and complements this book. Content includes video, audio, weblinks, quizzes, a slideshow, and activities.

AV² Online Navigation

Audio
Listen to sections of the book read aloud.

Book Pages
AV² pages directly correspond to pages in the book.

Video
Watch informative video clips.

Embedded Weblinks
Gain additional information for research.

Key Words
Study vocabulary, and complete a matching word activity.

Try This!
Complete activities and hands-on experiments.

Quizzes
Test your knowledge.

Slideshow
View images and captions, and prepare a presentation.

AV² was built to bridge the gap between print and digital. We encourage you to tell us what you like and what you want to see in the future.

Sign up to be an AV² Ambassador at www.av2books.com/ambassador.

Due to the dynamic nature of the internet, some of the URLs and activities provided as part of AV² by Weigl may have changed or ceased to exist. AV² by Weigl accepts no responsibility for any such changes. All media enhanced books are regularly monitored to update addresses and sites in a timely manner. Contact AV² by Weigl at 1-866-649-3445 or av2books@weigl.com with any questions, comments, or feedback.